1

HEALING FOR THE HURTING HEART

BY

NANCY JANE PIATT

INTRODUCTION

Sometimes, life just hurts. People are mean. Bad things happen. In those moments, God often uses simple and unexpected diversions to cause us to look up and remember who it is that is truly in control.

My prayer is that everyone who reads this book will find those unexpected blessings in the midst of their pain. There can be joy in sorrow; it's just not easy to see at times.

The best is yet to come.

✝

THE FIRE

Lights from a dozen fire trucks illuminated the evening sky as hundreds of people gathered to watch the firefighters battle the six alarm blaze. Flames were shooting high into the air, threatening to spread to nearby homes.

The fire had begun in the chimney and spread quickly without anyone knowing that danger was lurking. Its blazing fingers had traveled silently between the chimney walls and the siding on the outside of the house.

Finally, the intense heat and flames could no longer be contained, and flames burst through the top of the roof. A neighbor dialed 911, but the town that was home to the fiery menace was far from the nearest fire station.

After what seemed like hours a flurry of fire trucks began to arrive on the scene, carrying dozens of firefighters prepared for battle.

Friends, neighbors and people from the community gathered in stunned silence to watch as flames engulfed the tiny structure she called home. As she watched the firefighters work frantically to contain the blaze, she began to weep.

In a world where she was always the strong one, always the one with the answers, she now stood helpless, without the power to stop the impending disaster. She bowed her head, and with tears streaming down her face, she silently cried out to God.

"Lord, I don't know what to do. I can't stop this. I need you. I don't know what else to do, so I praise you."

It was almost as if the arms of God Himself wrapped around her, comforting her, protecting her. She was sure she heard Him whisper, "It's okay. I've got this."

Peace settled into her heart, and she smiled. He was there, even in this dark hour. The next days, weeks and months were filled with the aggravation of dealing with the loss of most of her personal possessions, as well as the rebuilding of her home.

Each day seemed to present a new challenge to be faced, another obstacle to be overcome. The peace of Christ carried her as she navigated the uncertain waters. She held close to her heart the sense of His presence when the fire seemed unstoppable.

She knew that, even in the face of devastation, He was there.

✝

THE FIRE, PART TWO

As soon as her fist hit the counter, she knew she was wrong. Frustration had been building up over the last several months, but she ignored the signs. Now, here, in the middle of the store, her anger lashed out onto a store manager over a delivery that had failed to show up for the third time.

The rest of the transaction was a blur. The manager accepted her feeble apology, but he was obviously offended, and rightfully so. He then scrambled around for nearly an hour trying to figure out what went wrong – again – and how to make it right this time.

Finally, she left the store, feeling deflated and defeated, with another promised delivery date in her hand. As she climbed into her car, she felt the hot sting of tears roll down her cheeks. These last several months had been almost more than she could bear. Nothing seemed to go right since the day the fire destroyed her home.

The fire happened on Memorial Day. Almost everything was gone. The insurance company was slow to process her claim, and the mortgage company would not release the money to the contractor so work could begin.

Now, six months after the disaster, construction had only just begun. It would be at least another six months before she could go home.

With the holidays rapidly approaching and so little progress made, she was feeling the strain of having been displaced from her life for so long. There were so many decisions to be made, and so many interruptions and distractions that she had not taken the time to even reflect on the meaning of Christmas.

As she tried to understand what had just happened in the store, she bowed her head in shame.

"Lord," she said softly. "I failed you. All you asked from me in this was that I trust you, and I couldn't do it. I'm sorry."

In the quiet, she sensed His presence. Her heart was at peace in spite of her failure. As she gratefully accepted His forgiveness, she heard His still, small voice whisper:

"That's why I came."

✝

CHRISTMAS VIGIL

A soft moan broke the silence in her room. She stirred briefly, and fell back into a deep sleep. I began to think about this woman I had hardly known – my mother.

The sounds of Christmas floated in from the hallway at the nursing home, muffled, but clear. I stared sadly at the tiny lights on the Christmas tree that adorned her dresser. Mom struggled with depression, and that kept her estranged and isolated from us as we grew up and moved on with our lives.

It had only been in the last few months since she became ill that I learned anything about who she really was. I began to think about how carefully God had orchestrated each and every moment of time that brought us to this very place.

This would not be my most festive holiday, for sure. There was no Christmas tree with presents under it, no brightly colored holiday decorations, and no smells of a turkey as it roasted in the oven. And yet, I knew this Christmas would be the most precious of all.

Mom became sick just three short months ago. The doctor said that Mom would get better eventually, and that she could even live for another twenty years or so. We had spent the last few months creating memories. We sat for hours as she talked about how she grew up, with me absorbing every word.

As she shared her life with me, I began to understand why her heart had become so burdened for so many years. By God's grace I began to love her for the mother she was able to be, instead of longing for the mother that I wanted her to be. I began to spend as much time with her as I could, and I had come to treasure those moments.

As the weeks went on, I began to suspect that something was not right. Mom was doing everything she was supposed to do, yet she still seemed very frail and weak. The doctor dismissed my concerns, telling me that Mom was older, and would take longer to recover.

It was the home care nurse who first recognized the signs. In just two short weeks everything changed when I met with the nurse on that fateful day. With gentleness and great strength, she looked into my eyes and said, "Your mother is dying, Nancy, and soon."

Mom accepted her fate gracefully. She spent time making decisions about her funeral and burial. She told me exactly how she wanted things to be done. Her final resting place was to be in Pennsylvania in the cemetery across from our old home. At her request, one week before Christmas – on my birthday - I made the four hour drive to the funeral home and finalized her funeral and burial arrangements.

We did not have many chances to talk after that as disease slowly robbed her of her strength. Still, I found out that she had professed Christ as her Savior when she was a little girl.

Although that took me completely by surprise, I was delighted. We knew we would see each other again, and that strengthened the bond we had only recently begun to build.

As I sat now, on Christmas Eve, I could hear muffled sounds of music and laughter. I began to cry out to God.

"Please, God, don't take her tonight. Just give us one more Christmas. Please…"

Tears streamed down my face as I watched her breathe, her chest slowly rising and falling, her face ashen. My body gave into fatigue and I drifted off to sleep as I gently cradled her hand in mine.

I woke up at about four in the morning. Silence. I looked over at my mother. Her eyes opened for just a moment. She tried to smile at me as our eyes met, then she turned her head slightly and drifted back to sleep.

"Thank you, God," I whispered as tears filled my eyes.

I closed my eyes and tried to sleep, but the sounds of the hustle and bustle of the nursing home soon made it impossible to rest. As the morning passed, I heard cries of "Merry Christmas!" and "Look what Santa brought me, Grandma!"

I smiled as I imagined their faces, bright with joy. All day long there was an endless stream of celebration outside my mother's room. As I listened to the beautiful sounds of love coming from those hallways, I thought about what God had given me for Christmas. Time. Another day with a woman I had only begun to truly know.

There will be other Christmas Days for me, Lord willing. There will be festive decorations, gifts wrapped with pretty paper and bows, and a feast prepared with joy. But this Christmas, God gave me a gift that will never fade away, never be forgotten. This year, He gave me one more precious day with my mother.

†

PRICELESS TREASURE

The line at the grocery store was long and uninviting. I wheeled my contentious shopping cart closer towards the mayhem. My son Michael, who was five at the time, had just discovered yet another item he absolutely needed.

Stress was slowly stealing what little patience I had left as I explained that we just could not afford to buy anything extra. Although he was disappointed, I could see in his face that this time, it was okay.

We took our place in the checkout line, watching as customers in front of us loaded their carefully chosen groceries and assorted sundries on the conveyor belt. Suddenly, Michael noticed the long row of candy, gumball and prize machines near the checkout counter.

With eyes wide with excitement, he fervently tugged on my dress.

"Please, Mommy, can I go look?"

How could I deny that passionate plea? With my blessing, a leap and a smile he headed off to explore the beckoning trinkets and treasures.

Exhaustion was finally taking its toll. Sleep had been eluding me since the break in at our apartment the week before. The sickening feeling in my stomach lingered for days as the events of that dreadful night kept replaying in my mind.

We had arrived home at our usual time that evening. Michael was chatting passionately about something that happened on the playground. As I turned the key to our apartment door, I noticed that it wasn't locked.

Did I leave our door unlocked? I wondered to myself. *What a careless mistake!*

As we entered our home, I saw that the trash had been dumped over and the bag was missing. Sighing, I walked over to clean up the mess. I automatically assumed that Michael emptied the trash on the floor. No doubt he needed the bag for reasons that would only make sense to an adventurous five year old.

He ran to the sofa and begged to watch a movie while I prepared our dinner. I wearily gave in and walked towards the television to load his selection into the VCR.

As I made my way over to the entertainment center, something didn't seem right. It took a few seconds for me to grasp what the problem was. Finally, I understood. *The VCR was missing!*

Lord, I thought to myself, *someone has broken into our home!*

The safe haven that we had created to shield us from the harsh realities of a cold world had been violated. I immediately called the police. While we waited for them to come we walked around the apartment looking to see what else was missing.

Michael's bright blue eyes were now clouded with fear. He would not leave my side. Line by line we made a list of all items that had been stolen on a notepad with Michael's favorite pen. A jar that I kept change in had been emptied. A clock radio and small stereo were also missing.

The thief also made off with a small stash of silver dollars and other cash that I had. I was devastated when I discovered that the intruder had stolen all of my jewelry.

Thankfully, the contents of Michael's room had been spared. I could not help but smile at Michael's exuberance upon discovering that the thief had not taken his dead bug collection.

When the detective finally arrived, we were able to calmly tell him what we found when we came home. Michael proudly presented the policeman with our list. The officer accepted it graciously, assuring Michael that he had been a very big help.

After taking fingerprints from the door and a few surfaces in the apartment, the detective and I spent a few minutes talking. His best guess was that the thief had used the trash bag to put the stolen items in. He said it was highly unlikely that anything that had been taken would be recovered.

In short, while this was devastating to us, as crimes go, this one was negligible. Disappointment taunted me as I thanked him and walked him to the door.

During dinner, Michael and I talked about what had happened. He was sad that we lost the VCR. He knew we would not be able to replace it for a very long time. That meant we could not have our special movie nights. It was a tough loss for a five year old boy.

We also talked about how we were going to try to not be afraid. We discussed the possibility of spending the night someplace else. Michael bravely decided we could sleep in our apartment. His only condition was that we pile things in front of the door so no one could come in. I was happy to oblige.

Now, a week later, neither of us was sleeping very well. Every day Michael had a new question about the robbery. We were both angry about what happened. We were also both a little afraid that it could happen again.

A screaming child brought my thoughts promptly back to the present. The checkout line was moving steadily forward. Finally I arrived at the counter. I emptied the contents of my shopping cart onto the conveyor belt and moved towards the cash register.

As I prepared to write a check, my son came running up to me, his face flushed bright red with excitement.

"Mommy, please," this blonde haired moppet begged excitedly. "Please, may I have a dime?"

His wide eyes cried out to me, proclaiming that this dime was for a truly significant treasure. How could I refuse? I placed the coin in his outstretched palm and he scurried off to secure his prize.

The clerk was handing over my receipt when Michael arrived back at the counter, his hand clutched tightly.

"Here, Mommy!" he said, beaming with great joy. He thrust his hand towards me with contagious delight. A ring made of orange plastic and tin sparkled in his little fingers. "Now you have some new jewelry."

Tears crept in my eyes as I accepted his gift. With a puzzled look, the cashier exclaimed, "How lovely!"

You have no idea, I thought to myself. I hugged my precious boy and thanked him for being so generous. I placed the ring on my finger and wore it proudly every day for the next several weeks. To me, it was a sign from God that we were going to be okay.

Many decades have passed since that tender moment. When I close my eyes I can still picture the smile on my little boy's face as he tenderly displayed the present he bought just for me. That ring is still in my jewelry box today.

Through the years I have received many presents that were bigger and more expensive than his simple gift. The stories behind them, as sweet as they are, pale in comparison to the memory that accompanies that priceless treasure.

✝

THAT'S WHY I CAME

He hung his head, ashamed that he had failed. He had let down his family, his friends, himself. Even worse, he sinned against God.

What hope do I have if I always fall? he wondered to himself. God hadn't asked much from him, after all. Just for him to be obedient. And he blew it.

He fell asleep with thoughts of condemnation tormenting him as he tried to rest. Images of his past mistakes haunted him, forcing him to run through the pages of his life hoping to escape the gruesome reminders of his imperfections.

Finally, he happened upon a little child. She took his hand gently and said, "Come with me, mister."

She led him down a narrow street paved with gold. They walked together silently, their footsteps echoing in the stillness. A sense of curiosity began to fill his troubled soul. As they traveled down the street, they came upon a man standing near the tablets upon which the Ten Commandments were etched.

"Do you know who that is?" the child asked, gazing intently upon his face.

"Sure. That's Moses," the man answered. "God gave him the Ten Commandments and used him to lead the Israelites out of Egypt."

"Yes. And Moses also killed an Egyptian," the girl replied solemnly.

They continued walking until they saw a man standing like a great warrior.

"Do you know who that is?" the child asked.

"That's David. He's called a man after God's own heart," the man answered. "He was a great king!"

"David committed adultery with Bathsheba," the child responded soberly. "Then he had her husband killed to try and cover up his sin."

They continued walking and a short while later they came upon Peter, one of the followers of Christ.

The man declared, "That's Peter! He was one of the twelve disciples!"

"Peter denied Jesus three times even though he said he would never deny his Lord," the little girl said sadly.

As she led him further down the road, they saw a woman about to be stoned. When the child asked if he knew who the woman was, the man told her the story of how the woman had been caught in adultery.

The law demanded that she be stoned to death, but Jesus said the person without sin should cast the first stone. He then knelt down and began writing in the sand, and one by one the people who were going to stone her turned and walked away.

Eventually they came to Paul. The man was sure that Paul was a great Christian. The little girl sadly shook her head.

"He hated Christians before Jesus saved him. He persecuted them and had many killed just because they loved Jesus."

The man began to realize that every person he had ever read about in the Bible had failed – some in *big* ways. Murder, adultery, fornication, stealing, pride, lying – every sin he could possibly think of plagued all men and women throughout history. He turned to the child and asked why God would allow that.

"God made man in His image," the child said. "But man decided he wanted free will. Free will led to sin, and sin led to death. The only way

God could save man from himself was through a blood sacrifice. Jesus gave up His place in Heaven to walk among men to be that blood sacrifice."

The man fell into a deeper sleep, with the words of the child echoing through his mind. Finally in his anguish he woke up. With tears streaming down his face he cried out to God.

"God, I've tried to be a good Christian, but I just can't. I always seem to fall. If David, Peter and Paul failed, and they loved you the way they did, what hope is there for me?"

Suddenly, the room filled with a bright light. The man sat up and stared in wonder, unable to utter a sound. Standing in front of him was Jesus, smiling at him with a look of deep love in His eyes.

Jesus held out His arms, showing the man the scars on His

hands where the nails had been pounded into His flesh to hold Him on the cross. A tear rolled down His cheek as he gathered the man in His arms.

"That's why I came, my child," He said gently. "That's why I came."

†

THE BEST IS YET TO COME

Years had passed since Ann had spoken to her father. The argument that finally divided them so long ago seemed pointless now, in the face of his impending death.

Why didn't I call him? she thought, anguished at the thought of all those lost years. *Why didn't I just come back home?* Tears streamed down her face. She sobbed as she recalled the last few months before she left home for good.

Her mother had been the delight of her father's world. Ann recalled the look in his eyes every time he watched her mother walk into a room. She smiled sadly. When her mother passed away suddenly, it was if the joy that she brought into his life had been buried with her.

Weeks and months passed quickly after the funeral. Every day her father sank deeper and deeper into depression. He became more and more demanding and impossible to be with. Ann could not remember the last time she saw him smile. Finally, his meanness had pushed her to the limit.

"I never want to see you again!" she had shouted at him as she slammed the door to their tiny ranch house.

She ran to her car and drove off, vowing to never look back. And for three years she never did. Until yesterday, when his neighbor called to tell her that he was dying and she should come home.

When she pulled her car into the driveway, she noticed the drapes were all open, unlike the last time she was here. Back then, the drapes were always closed, as if her father was trying to keep the world out.

That's odd, she thought. Ann stepped out of her car and slowly walked to the door. She wondered if she should ring the bell. Was she welcome here anymore?

A hundred questions swirled around in her mind. She raised her hand to knock. Before her knuckles hit the hard wood, the door flung open wide and Patricia, their next door neighbor stood in the entrance, a sad smile on her face.

"Welcome home, Ann dear!" Patricia exclaimed. "Your father will be so happy to see you!"

Ann hugged the matronly woman.

"How is he, Miss Patricia?" she asked pensively. "What happened?"

"Well, now, your father has cancer," Patricia said gently. "The doctor said he doesn't have long. There isn't anything they can do for him, so he wanted to come home. He's asleep now. He's been sleeping a lot lately, but he's not in much pain."

"Why didn't he call me?" Ann cried out.

"Now, honey," Patricia replied as she led Ann into the kitchen. "He just found out three weeks ago. He's been putting his affairs in order so you won't have to worry about anything when he's gone. He'll be so happy to see you."

Ann fought back the tears. She sat down at the kitchen table. Memories of happier times flooded her mind. She closed her eyes and pictured her mom and dad laughing at dinner. She adored the way they used to look at each other. Why did that have to end?

Patricia poured tea and placed a plate of cookies on the table. They talked for an hour reminiscing about happier times.

"This house is so beautiful with the sunlight pouring in. Thank you for opening the curtains, Patricia," Ann said finally. "My dad never wanted them open after my mom died."

"Oh, sweetheart," Patricia said, slightly surprised. "Your father insisted I leave them all open – even in his bedroom! When he came home from the hospital last week, he started cleaning up around the house. I was very surprised when he asked me for help."

Ann thought about Patricia's words. She was right – her father never asked for help. *He really is sick,* she thought to herself. She tried to prepare herself for the worst.

"I'd like to sit with him until he wakes up," Ann said sadly.

"Of course, honey," Patricia replied graciously. "There's a chair right by the bed. He's been hoping you would come."

As she walked slowly down the hall to his room, Ann wondered what to say to him. Was he angry because of the way she left? Would he really be happy to see her, or was this just another chance for him to take his anger out on her?

Fear started to creep into her heart. She took a deep breath and slowly opened the door. Sunlight danced off the curtains and playfully hovered on the bed where he lay fast asleep.

A Bible rested on the night stand next to the lamp. Ann couldn't remember the last time she had seen him read the Bible after her mom died. Quietly she made her way over to the chair and sat down.

She wondered how long he would sleep. After a few minutes she picked up the Bible and began to flip through the pages. A letter fell onto the floor. Ann leaned over to retrieve it.

The envelope was old and faded, but the handwriting was clearly feminine. It was addressed to "My Prince" – her mother's pet name for her father. Ann smiled. She could almost hear her mother's voice telling her that her Prince was coming home.

She gently turned the letter over and over in her hands. Should she read it? *No,* she thought to herself. *It's a private thing between them.* She laid the envelope on the night stand and flipped through the Bible again.

Finally, curiosity won and she pulled the letter from the envelope and began to read. Her mother had written it right after they were married. As she read her mother's private thoughts, Ann thought about how tender and sweet their love for each other was. *This is beautiful,* she thought.

She turned the yellowed page over and began to read the other side. Tears filled her eyes as she realized why her father had changed his mind about the curtains.

Someday, my Prince, her mother had written all those years ago, *someday one of us will die and leave the other one behind for a little while. Promise me that if I go first, you will always remember the beauty of the day we danced in the sunlight.*

Dance with joy. Laugh. Love our children. And always remember that the best is yet to come. This life is not all there is. I will wait for you then just as I did when you were in the Navy. We will be together again. The best is yet to come!

"I'm so sorry, Princess," her father said, his voice weak and raspy. "I didn't mean to make you go away."

Ann looked into her father's pale face. Her heart wrenched at the sadness in his eyes.

"Oh, Daddy!" she replied gently. "I'm sorry for leaving that way! I love you!"

She leaned down and kissed his cheek. He wrapped his arms tenderly around her. Ann could tell how weak he was now. She knew there wasn't much time left.

"I read Mom's letter, Daddy," Ann whispered. "It's so beautiful! She loved you so much!"

Too weary to keep his arms elevated, her father slowly let them fall to his sides. Ann laid her head on his shoulder and rested her arm across his chest.

"I'd forgotten all about that letter," he said softly, his eyes shining with love. "I forgot about the day we danced in the sunlight. She's waiting for me, you know!"

"I know, Daddy," Ann said sadly as she felt the life leave his body. Tears flowed freely as she quietly sobbed.

"The best is yet to come!"

✝

www.ingramcontent.com/pod-product-compliance
Lightning Source LLC
Chambersburg PA
CBHW060633030426
42337CB00018B/3338